UNCOMMON MARRIAGE

BIBLE STUDY

TONY & LAUREN
DUNGY

WITH NATHAN WHITAKER
AND STEPHANIE RISCHE

TYNDALE™
MOMENTUM

An Imprint of Tyndale House Publishers, Inc.

Visit Tyndale online at www.tyndale.com.

Visit Tyndale Momentum online at www.tyndalemomentum.com.

TYNDALE is a registered trademark of Tyndale House Publishers, Inc. *Tyndale Momentum* and the Tyndale Momentum logo are trademarks of Tyndale House Publishers, Inc. Tyndale Momentum is an imprint of Tyndale House Publishers, Inc.

UnCommon is a trademark of Tyndale House Publishers, Inc.

Uncommon Marriage Bible Study

Designed by Dean Renninger

Published in association with the literary agency of Legacy, LLC, Winter Park, Florida 32789.

Printed in the United States of America

ISBN 978-1-4143-9199-1

20 19 18 17 16 15 14
 7   6   5   4   3   2   1

CONTENTS

A NOTE FROM THE DUNGYS

Welcome to Your Journey to an Uncommon Marriage

We are so glad you have joined us on this adventure to an uncommon marriage! After more than thirty years together, we are still learning about marriage, about each other, and about God's desires for us as a couple. We've been through a lot—big victories, devastating losses, and everything in between. But through it all we've experienced God's faithfulness. We've witnessed firsthand that His plan for marriage is good, and we're eager to share a few of the things He's taught us along the way.

Over the years we've mentored a number of couples—including friends from church and young football players and their wives—and we've also shared some of our marriage journey with the members of the small group that meets at our home. We wish our living room were big enough to invite all of you over to talk about marriage and the good things God has planned for you and your spouse.

But since there would be some logistical issues with that, we'd like to invite you to join us on the pages of this study instead.

May the Lord bless you as you grow deeper in your marriage and strengthen your bond with the teammate God has given you.

Tony and Lauren Dungy

Two people are better off than one, for they can help each other succeed. If one person falls, the other can reach out and help.
ECCLESIASTES 4:9-10

HOW TO USE THIS BIBLE STUDY

This five-week study is designed to be used in a variety of ways: in a small group setting, in a men's or women's study, in conjunction with a church-wide campaign, or one-on-one with your spouse.

To get the most out of this study, you will need a Bible and the book *Uncommon Marriage*, which tells the story of the Dungys' marriage and provides the context for the questions and discussion topics in this book. (Please note that the chapter numbers that follow quotes from Tony and Lauren in this study tell you where to find that passage in *Uncommon Marriage*.)

Although the book and the study can be used separately, you will benefit most from the experience if you use these resources in conjunction. This study includes suggested readings from *Uncommon Marriage* to correspond with each week's session.

Here are a few ideas about how you can implement this Bible study in a variety of contexts.

IN A COUPLES' SMALL GROUP

You may want to participate in this study with a small group, with several sets of friends, or with a Sunday school class. The ideal group size is three to six couples, but depending on the format of your group, you could also meet as a larger group for part of the discussion and then break into smaller groups for sharing and prayer. Some groups meet on a weekly basis; others find it works better to meet every other week. You can determine the schedule that best suits the needs of your group.

IN A MEN'S OR WOMEN'S STUDY

Another option is to go through this study in an all-men's or an all-women's small group. This approach may be a good option for gender-specific classes that meet in churches or for informal groups of friends. Additional content specific to men and women is available online at coachdungy.com.

AS A CHURCH

If you are interested in using *Uncommon Marriage* as a church-wide campaign, go to coachdungy.com, where you can access information and resources to help you implement this series at your church. You'll find sermon notes, tips for leaders, promotional materials, and video trailers so your entire congregation can focus on building healthy marriages as a community.

AS A COUPLE

You may want to go through this study one-on-one with your spouse. The content is relevant regardless of the stage of your relationship—whether you've been married for years, are newlyweds, or are engaged to be married. It may be helpful to set aside specific times to discuss the questions to ensure that you have a chance to engage with the material together.

WHAT EACH SESSION INCLUDES

Before Your Session: Tells you which chapters to read in *Uncommon Marriage* and informs you of anything else you need to do to prepare for the session.

Getting Started: Offers an icebreaker to spark conversation and set a comfortable tone for group meetings.

Building an Uncommon Marriage: Guides your group through discussion questions based on the Dungys' experiences and the book *Uncommon Marriage.*

Looking at God's Word: Provides relevant Scripture verses to help you understand and apply what God says about the topics addressed in the session.

Wrapping Up: Helps you focus on takeaway points you want to remember and apply in the week ahead.

On Your Own: Gives you and your spouse connecting points and questions to discuss after the session.

May God work in these next five weeks to help you grow as a group, as a community, as a church . . . and especially as a couple.

AN UNCOMMON FOUNDATION

//

BEFORE YOUR FIRST SESSION

Read chapters 1–3 of *Uncommon Marriage*; find a wedding photo to share with the group.

GETTING STARTED

Where It All Began

If possible, bring a wedding photo to your first session. Allow time for everyone to share their photos, and then discuss the following questions.

What was the biggest disaster or something that didn't go as planned on your wedding day?

What is a special memory from your wedding?

BUILDING AN UNCOMMON MARRIAGE

Making Decisions Together

Practically from the moment they say "I do," every couple is faced with the daunting task of merging two sets of opinions into one unified decision. Where will we live? How will we spend our vacations? How often will we see family? Which way will we hang the toilet-paper roll? Some decisions are life changing; others are mundane, but whatever the issue, being able to communicate well when making decisions together is essential to having a healthy marriage.

Tony says, "Early on, we learned to ask God for two things when praying about decisions: first, that He would give us His infinite wisdom and direction, and second, that He would put us on the same page. Over the years, we've come to realize that when we are frustrated with each other, it's because we haven't spent enough time praying or communicating about spiritual matters to understand each other's heart on something" (ch. 2).

1. When you're facing a big decision, how do you usually go about making it? Are you an internal processor, or would you rather talk through everything? Are there certain people you go to for input or advice? Do you rely on your gut feeling? Do you make a list of pros and cons?

2. How does your decision-making style differ from your spouse's? How have you learned to work together with your different wirings?

3. When Tony and Lauren were seeking God's will about whether they should move to one of the big-city teams or to the Kansas City Chiefs, there was no "booming voice from the sky" clearly telling them which way to go. Ultimately, though, they sensed that Kansas City was the right fit for their family. Do you and your spouse seek God's will in your decision making? If so, what does that look like? What are some ways you might be more intentional about doing that?

Dealing with Change

The Dungys experience a number of significant transitions in these first three chapters, including bringing foster children into their home, having two children of their own, starting a new job, and making a major move away from family. Some changes in marriage are anticipated and planned, while others come as a surprise and may be entirely beyond our control. Either way, change can rock a relationship, prompting a couple to either drift apart or lean in toward each other.

Sometimes a major life change can happen in a single moment. This was the case for the Dungys when Tony announced he was thinking of leaving the Steelers after being asked to take a demotion. Lauren says, "It was painful, even though Tony pointed out that this might be the Lord's way of moving us along. That didn't make it any easier. And, by the way, where was He moving us? We had no idea" (ch. 3).

4. What significant changes have you faced since you've been together?

5. In what ways have those changes drawn you closer together? In what ways have they threatened to pull you apart?

Making Sacrifices

In his book *Mere Christianity*, C. S. Lewis describes love as "a deep unity, maintained by the will and deliberately strengthened by habit; reinforced by [in Christian marriages] the grace which both partners ask, and receive, from God."[*] Early in their relationship, Lauren and Tony realized that marriage isn't just about feelings; it's about the decisions a couple make to remain unified and committed to each other even when they don't necessarily feel like it.

When it came time to move away from Pittsburgh, Lauren and Tony both made sacrifices for the greater good of the family. Lauren chose to support her husband even when it meant moving away from her family, friends, and church home: "I was crying and very emotional, but I told Tony I would support him either way. If he wanted to look for another job, I didn't mind moving. That was the sacrifice you made for life in football. I was in it with him" (ch. 3). Tony, too, made sacrifices by putting his family ahead of his career. Joining the staff of the San Francisco 49ers would have been a good career move, but he chose what was best for his children instead: "[The 49ers] wanted me to coach offense, which would have broadened my horizons professionally. Yet the team's location, a big city

---

[*] Sources for quotations from anyone other than the Dungys are provided on page 107.

on the West Coast, didn't seem right to me because of where we were as a young family" (ch. 3).

6. What are some of the sacrifices—big or small—that you've made for your spouse or for your family?

7. What couple do you admire for the godly sacrifices they've made for each other or for their children? What is the most significant lesson you've learned from them?

Building a Spiritual Foundation

The Dungys talk about the importance of establishing a healthy spiritual foundation as a couple. Many of the habits they formed at the beginning of their relationship, such as going to church together, praying together, connecting spiritually, and seeking God's wisdom, are patterns they have hung on to throughout their marriage. These routines have endured as they've entered new life stages and faced difficult seasons.

Whether you're nearing your wedding day or you've been married for a while, it's never too late to be intentional about incorporating habits like these into your relationship.

8. Tony says, "If I had to name the number one thing that got our marriage off to a great start, it was finding the right church home. It provided a solid foundation for us as a newlywed couple" (ch. 2). How important do you think finding a church home is to building a foundation in marriage?

9. In this season of your life, what qualities must a church have to be the right fit for your family—to be a true "church home"?

10. Tony and Lauren emphasize the importance of having a strong vertical relationship (with the Lord) and a strong horizontal relationship (with each other): "We established the habit of spending time talking about God—and to God—together" (ch. 2). What are some ways you've seen other couples you respect connect spiritually?

11. What habits have you established as a couple to connect spiritually? What are some habits you'd like to incorporate more regularly into your marriage?

Keep in mind that there isn't one right formula for this. The way you connect with each other and with God may look different from the way other couples connect, and the specifics may differ depending on your season of life and unique circumstances. Don't feel pressure to fit into a certain mold; the important thing is to be intentional about nurturing your spiritual bond as a vital part of your relationship.

LOOKING AT GOD'S WORD

Read these Scripture passages and discuss what they mean to you.

Making Decisions Together

Trust in the LORD with all your heart;
*   do not depend on your own understanding.*
Seek his will in all you do,
*   and he will show you which path to take.*
PROVERBS 3:5-6

Whether you turn to the right or to the left, your ears will hear
a voice behind you, saying, "This is the way; walk in it."
ISAIAH 30:21, NIV

What do you think it means to seek God's will and "not depend on your own understanding" (Proverbs 3:5)? What are some ways you might be more intentional about doing that?

The Bible tells us that God's voice is real and will guide us as we walk through life (Isaiah 30:21, NIV). What are some of the ways you have heard God's voice in your life?

Dealing with Change

Your kingdom is an everlasting kingdom.
  You rule throughout all generations.

The LORD always keeps his promises;
  he is gracious in all he does.
PSALM 145:13

Jesus Christ is the same yesterday, today, and forever.
HEBREWS 13:8

Though change can rock our lives, the Lord and His love are the same "yesterday, today, and forever"

(Hebrews 13:8). How could this perspective affect the way you and your spouse respond to change as a couple?

Making Sacrifices

There is no greater love than to lay down one's life for one's friends.
JOHN 15:13

Don't be selfish; don't try to impress others. Be humble, thinking of others as better than yourselves. Don't look out only for your own interests, but take an interest in others, too.
PHILIPPIANS 2:3-4

The Bible instructs us to think of "others as better than [ourselves]" and to "take an interest in others, too" (Philippians 2:3-4). How do you demonstrate that you think well of and take an interest in your spouse?

Practically speaking, how might you implement other principles from the Scripture passages in this section in your marriage and family life?

Building a Spiritual Foundation

You must commit yourselves wholeheartedly to these commands that I am giving you today. Repeat them again and again to your children. Talk about them when you are at home and when you are on the road, when you are going to bed and when you are getting up.
DEUTERONOMY 6:6-7

Christ will make his home in your hearts as you trust in him. Your roots will grow down into God's love and keep you strong.
EPHESIANS 3:17

An important part of building a spiritual foundation is committing yourself wholeheartedly to God's commands (Deuteronomy 6:6-7). What do you think it would look like for you and your spouse to do this?

In Ephesians, Paul says that when Christ enters our hearts, our roots "grow down into God's love" and keep us strong (3:17). Why do you think it's so important to have a strong spiritual foundation together as a couple?

WRAPPING UP

What's one takeaway from this session you would like to focus on as a couple or as a family in the week ahead?

How can the rest of the group pray for you?

ON YOUR OWN

(To be completed after the session.)

Set aside some time to spend as a couple in the week ahead. Try to find about fifteen minutes away from other distractions to apply what you learned in this session to your relationship.

* Is there something you would like to start doing to connect with each other spiritually (praying together, reading the Bible together, attending a Bible class, talking about spiritual things, etc.)? What might it look like to build this habit into your life?

* If you haven't found a church home, make a list of the things you're looking for in a church and then plan how you will find the right one. (You might start by talking to friends for suggestions and looking online for churches in your area.)

* If you already have a church home, are there ways you'd like to plug in more and make connections? Are there ways you could be using your gifts there? How could you be intentional about building authentic community?

* Spend some time praying together. Ask God to give you wisdom as you make decisions, to help you build a strong foundation for your marriage, to trust Him in the midst of life changes, and to cultivate a relationship marked by selflessness.

AN UNCOMMON OUTLOOK

//

BEFORE YOUR SECOND SESSION

Read chapters 4–6 of *Uncommon Marriage*. Designate one person in the group to bring a Nerf football or another ball that's soft and easy to catch.

GETTING STARTED

Getting to Know You Game

For this activity, you will need a Nerf football or another easy-to-catch ball. When a group member is holding the ball, have him or her answer one of the following questions. After the first person has answered the question, he or she can toss it to someone else until everyone in the group has had a turn.

What stood out to you most about your spouse on the day you first met him or her?

What couple on a TV show do you enjoy watching? What about their relationship is relatable or entertaining?

What married couple from real life do you admire? What is it about their relationship that you appreciate?

BUILDING AN UNCOMMON MARRIAGE

Making Time for Each Other

When Tony took a new job with the Kansas City Chiefs, his family faced a number of new challenges. One big adjustment was the intense work schedule and the expectation that the coaches would stay late in the evenings. Tony and Lauren realized that with such considerable demands on their time, they would need to be intentional about making time to connect as a couple and as a family. One of the priorities they set during this season was to make sure they got away from work and distractions regularly to spend time together—usually by walking or riding their bicycles.

We all struggle with demands on our schedules, whether because of work, classes, church commitments, community involvement, house maintenance, or children's activities. Even good things can threaten to steal our time with our loved ones, and all too often the people we care for most get the leftovers. That's why it's critical for us to set aside time to spend together and then to guard those moments vigilantly.

1. What are some activities you enjoy doing as a couple and/or a family?

2. What distractions are most likely to keep you from spending time with your spouse and/or children?

3. What boundaries could you put in place to protect time with your loved ones?

Leadership and Submission in Marriage

According to author Mike Mason, "Couples who submit wholeheartedly in marriage, both to God and to one another, stand on the threshold of paradise, of pure bliss." The topic of submission and leadership in marriage can often be a loaded one, but this conversation isn't intended to spark controversy about gender roles; it's meant to help you focus on your own relationship and the gifts and callings God has given each of you.

Tony offers his perspective on what it means for a husband to be a leader in a marriage: "I've watched some men get annoyed when their wives take the lead in any area of their homes. I think that's shortsighted. As Chuck Noll used to tell his coaches, our job was to help the players play the best they could. So I can't look at my marriage and think, *My job is to be the head coach and make the rules, and Lauren's job is to make sure my rules are being followed.* No, our job in marriage is to help the house function as well as it can and to raise our kids in the best way possible" (ch. 4).

4. What do you think it means for a husband to be a leader in his marriage? How has this idea of leadership in marriage played out in your relationship?

Lauren emphasizes the importance of communication but acknowledges that sometimes when she and Tony were making decisions, they had differences of opinion. In those situations, she says she made an intentional choice to submit to him: "When Tony and I don't view a situation in the same way, I believe I have to follow what the Bible says about marital roles and let Tony know, 'I feel strongly about this, but we're going to do what you think is best. As the husband and father of our home, you bear the primary responsibility to lead in our home.' That doesn't mean I stuff down my feelings or put on an artificial smile. I am open with Tony about my disappointment, but I don't allow myself to hang on to bitterness or resentment" (ch. 6).

5. What do you think submission means? What does it *not* mean?

6. When you've reached an impasse when making a decision as a couple, how do you handle it?

Seeing the Good

At some point in marriage, every couple will face a critical decision: Will they resent their spouse for their unfavorable circumstances, or will they remain united even in the face of something they wouldn't have chosen?

For Tony and Lauren, this point of decision came after their move from Kansas City to Minnesota. Lauren felt lonely there. She lacked the community she'd had in previous places they'd lived, and she struggled with the long, cold Minnesota winters. During this season, Lauren and Tony made sure they stayed focused on resolving the problems, not on who was right, when they faced conflict.

Lauren says, "We've learned that it's not always necessary to figure out who is wrong when we disagree. Instead, we try to think about an issue from the other person's point of view. Then we talk about how to resolve a situation in the best way—which is not necessarily my way or Tony's way" (ch. 6).

7. When disagreements arise, why do you think most of us have a tendency to focus on proving we're right instead of on solving the problem?

Lauren felt the seed of bitterness creeping in as she was tempted to blame Tony for making the decision to move to Minnesota, but eventually she realized that her critical feelings were only serving to drive a wedge between them: "The biggest lesson I learned was that complaining wasn't the way to go. In this instance, I had no reason to assign fault to Tony for my unhappiness" (ch. 6).

8. Tell about a time you found yourself in a set of circumstances that made you feel resentful or prone to complaining.

9. What helps you move toward a spirit of gratitude when you're in circumstances you wouldn't have chosen?

Encouraging Each Other

One of the blessings of marriage is that God gave you a built-in encourager in the form of your spouse. It can be a true gift to have someone by your side when you face setbacks or disappointments. But encouragement isn't something that spills out automatically for most people. Husbands and wives need to be intentional about recognizing when their spouse is down and then make the effort to encourage him or her. Lauren says, "I was coming to realize that the Lord had been testing my faith throughout our years in Minnesota. Tony had had some disappointments in his career, but this was really the first time I struggled with discouragement" (ch. 6).

Tony, too, relied on Lauren's encouragement when he was passed over for head coaching positions while still in Minnesota: "Letdowns like that are why God gave me a wife. I needed to hear Lauren tell me that she loved me and believed in me no matter what. And that's what she did" (ch. 6).

10. Tell about a time you felt discouraged and your spouse did something to lift your spirits.

LOOKING AT GOD'S WORD

Read these Scripture passages and discuss what they mean to you.

Making Time for Each Other

Jesus said, "Let's go off by ourselves to a quiet place and rest awhile." He said this because there were so many people coming and going that Jesus and his apostles didn't even have time to eat.
MARK 6:31

Those who won't care for their relatives, especially those in their own household, have denied the true faith. Such people are worse than unbelievers.
1 TIMOTHY 5:8

Even Jesus made time and space in his busy schedule to care for those He loved (Mark 6:31). Why do you think it's so important to set aside time for your spouse and/or family? Why do you think Jesus set an example for us in this?

Leadership and Submission in Marriage

Submit to one another out of reverence for Christ. For wives, this means submit to your husbands as to the Lord. . . . For husbands, this means love your wives, just as Christ loved the church. He gave up his life for her.
EPHESIANS 5:21-22, 25

Wives, submit to your husbands, as is fitting for those who belong to the Lord. Husbands, love your wives and never treat them harshly.
COLOSSIANS 3:18-19

What do you think it means for a husband to love his wife "as Christ loved the church" (Ephesians 5:25)? What would it look like for you or your spouse to put this into practice in your relationship?

What do you think the apostle Paul means when he tells women to submit to their husbands "as to the Lord"? How does he make clear that this does not mean husbands should treat their wives harshly or in a domineering way?

Seeing the Good

Fix your thoughts on what is true, and honorable, and right, and pure, and lovely, and admirable. Think about things that are excellent and worthy of praise.
PHILIPPIANS 4:8

Be thankful in all circumstances, for this is God's will for you who belong to Christ Jesus.
I THESSALONIANS 5:18

What do you think it means for us to fix our thoughts on "what is true and honorable, and right, and pure, and lovely, and admirable" (Philippians 4:8)? How can you practice this even in a frustrating situation?

The Bible tells us to "be thankful in all circumstances" (1 Thessalonians 5:18). What helps you move toward a spirit of gratitude when you're in circumstances you wouldn't have chosen?

Encouraging Each Other

Don't use foul or abusive language. Let everything you say be good and helpful, so that your words will be an encouragement to those who hear them.
EPHESIANS 4:29

Encourage each other and build each other up, just as you are already doing.
I THESSALONIANS 5:11

The Bible says we are to "encourage each other and build each other up" (1 Thessalonians 5:11). How can you be on the lookout for ways to encourage your spouse?

Practically speaking, how could you implement some of the principles from these verses in your marriage and family life?

WRAPPING UP

What's one takeaway from this session you would like to focus on as a couple or as a family in the week ahead?

How can the rest of the group pray for you?

ON YOUR OWN

(To be completed after the session.)

* Make a list of activities you enjoy doing together. Choose one thing you can do this week, and put it on the calendar. Place the list somewhere you'll see it often, and be intentional about setting aside time to spend together.

* Confess any areas where you've felt resentful or had a complaining attitude toward your spouse, and then ask for his or her forgiveness.

* Write a note of encouragement to your spouse when he or she faces a tough day in the week ahead.

AN UNCOMMON PARTNERSHIP

//

BEFORE YOUR THIRD SESSION

Read chapters 7–9 of *Uncommon Marriage*.

GETTING STARTED

The Battle of the Sexes

If you're part of a couples' small group, gather the women on one side of the room and the men on the other. Designate one person from the women's team who will ask questions of the men, and one person from the men's team to ask questions of the women. Take turns asking the questions below, and see how many questions each team gets right by working together as a group.

If you're part of a men's or women's group, divide the participants into two groups. Let one group ask the other group the first six questions; then let the second group quiz the first group on the remaining questions. After all the questions have been answered, see which team got more answers correct. (Leaders, please see page 106.)

1. *For the women:* Which of the following athletes was not an NFL MVP?

   a. Dan Marino
   b. Bill Russell
   c. Emmitt Smith
   d. Johnny Unitas

2. *For the men:* Which of the following athletes was not an Olympic figure skater?

   a. Dorothy Hamill
   b. Michelle Kwan
   c. Tara Lipinski
   d. Shannon Miller

3. *For the women:* Which of the following carpentry tools would you use to measure the distance between two opposite sides of an object?

a. calipers
b. clamp
c. jig
d. sliding bevel

4. *For the men:* Which of the following cooking techniques would you use to make bananas Foster?

a. brining
b. broasting
c. flambéing
d. parboiling

5. *For the women:* Which of the following cars does not have a V12 engine?

a. Bugatti
b. Ferrari
c. Rolls-Royce
d. Volkswagen Beetle

6. *For the men:* Which dance position means to bend at the knees?

   a. écart

   b. elevé

   c. plié

   d. pirouette

7. *For the women:* In hockey, what do you call a player with an accurate shot who often scores from a distance?

   a. cherry picker

   b. grinder

   c. slapper

   d. sniper

8. *For the men:* What do you call a sweater that has a wide swooping neck?

   a. A-line

   b. boat neck

   c. cowl neck

   d. turtleneck

9. *For the women:* Which of the following is not a baseball movie?

   a. *The Natural*

   b. *Miracle*

    c. *The Bad News Bears*
    d. *Angels in the Outfield*

10. *For the men:* Which of the following novels is not by Jane Austen?
    a. *Emma*
    b. *Little Women*
    c. *Sense and Sensibility*
    d. *Pride and Prejudice*

BUILDING AN UNCOMMON MARRIAGE

Setting Priorities

You don't have to be an NFL coach or a coach's wife to know what it's like to have a calendar crammed with commitments. Every day we are bombarded by so many things that scream for our attention, and it's easy for our families to get pushed to the side in the midst of the busyness.

When the Dungys were in Florida and started getting more public exposure, they found that even good things, like ministry opportunities, luncheons, speaking engagements, and requests to speak with the media, had the potential to pull their family apart. They quickly recognized that they would have to make some tough choices to keep their priorities in line. Lauren says, "As the number of requests increased, we realized how important it is to be discerning, because the good can quickly become the enemy of the best. We discovered that it can be hard to understand what the Lord wants in your life. He brings many opportunities, but we have to decide which ones will be most significant, what will most benefit the Kingdom of God, and what the costs will be. Tony and I talked a lot about maintaining our priorities—God, each other, our children, and then other important causes" (ch. 9).

1. How do you feel about the balance of your family's commitments right now? Are there some things you may need to start saying no to?

2. Some priorities for Tony and Lauren during this season of their lives were setting aside date nights, making sure their children's sports and other activities took precedence over outside causes, and taking time to pray together. What are some things you'd like to make more time for?

Being a Team

In his book *The Meaning of Marriage*, Timothy Keller talks about the power that comes from being part of a committed marriage: "When over the years someone has seen you at your worst . . . yet commits him- or herself to you wholly, it is a consummate experience. . . . To be fully known and truly loved is, well, a lot like being loved by God." Ultimately, a strong marriage isn't that different from a healthy sports team. Both are committed to the greater good, to the success of the whole.

When the Dungys first moved to Tampa Bay, they both found satisfying ways to use their gifts for a common goal. Lauren says, "One reason I enjoyed my work with the Bucs was that it gave me and Tony a sense that we were accomplishing something important together. Even though Tony had more responsibilities and was busier than ever, it didn't seem like it because we shared common goals" (ch. 8). Lauren and Tony were learning more about how to share in each other's passions and desires. Lauren continued to gain an appreciation for football, and Tony caught her vision for adding to their family through adoption.

3. Have you gained an appreciation for any of your spouse's interests or passions over the years? Explain.

4. Describe a situation when you and your spouse had a common vision and then worked successfully toward that goal together.

Playing to Your Strengths

Each player on a sports team has his or her own skills and set of experiences, and in most cases it would be detrimental to force a quarterback into a linebacker position or to ask a kicker to catch touchdown passes. In the same way, God has wired you and your spouse with unique strengths. You aren't the same—but that's actually a good thing.

In their marriage, Tony and Lauren embrace the roles they believe God has called them to as a husband and a wife, but they are careful not to let their relationship be defined by gender stereotypes. Lauren says, "We learned that operating as a unit didn't mean we had to let tradition define who did what in our household. I dislike using the words *strengths* and *weaknesses*, but there are some things that Tony is more gifted at doing and others that I feel I am better equipped to do. The key is working together to ensure we're each handling those things we do best" (ch. 8).

5. What are some of the jobs you and your spouse do that break stereotypical gender roles?

6. Describe an area of weakness for you that is an area of strength for your spouse.

Embracing Differences

If a choir were made up of all sopranos or all altos, it would lose the depth and texture of the different parts. In the same way, God designed our differences not to drive us crazy but to let us blend together in harmonies that are richer than what we could create on our own. Billy Graham describes marriage this way: "There is some merit to a description I once read of a married couple as 'happily incompatible.' Ruth likes to say, 'If two people agree on everything, one of them is unnecessary.' The sooner we accept that as a fact of life, the better we will be able to adjust to each other and enjoy togetherness."

When it comes to personalities, Tony and Lauren have noticed some key differences between them. While Tony tends to be more laid-back and levelheaded, Lauren considers herself to be more emotional and ready to act. Although those differences can cause stress, they can also complement each other in a beautiful way: "Over the course of our marriage, we've come to realize that our differences lead to a balance that is good, not bad. . . . God had brought us together, not despite our differences, but because of them" (ch. 9).

7. What are some of the traits that attracted you to your spouse as you started getting to know him or her?

8. What are some of the ways you and your spouse's personalities differ?

LOOKING AT GOD'S WORD

Read these Scripture passages and discuss what they mean to you.

Setting Priorities

The most important commandment is this: "Listen, O Israel! The LORD our God is the one and only LORD. And you must love the LORD your God with all your heart, all your soul, all your mind, and all your strength." The second is equally important: "Love your neighbor as yourself."
MARK 12:29-31

Choose today whom you will serve. . . . As for me and my family, we will serve the LORD.
JOSHUA 24:15

No matter your season in life, your first priority should always be to "love the LORD your God with all your heart, all your soul, all your mind, and all your strength" (Mark 12:30). What do you think it means to love God with all of your everything?

By choosing where to devote your time, you are choosing "whom [or what] you will serve" (Joshua 24:15).

How do you feel about the balance of your family's commitments right now? Are there some things you may need to start saying no to?

Being a Team

The LORD God said, "It is not good for the man to be alone. I will make a helper who is just right for him."
GENESIS 2:18

A man leaves his father and mother and is joined to his wife, and the two are united into one.
EPHESIANS 5:31

In Genesis, God creates Eve as "a helper who is just right" (2:18). What do you think this means for couples today?

In marriage, "two are united into one" (Ephesians 5:31). What do you think it means to be "one" with your spouse?

Playing to Your Strengths

God works in different ways, but it is the same God who does the work in all of us.
I CORINTHIANS 12:6

God has given each of you a gift from his great variety of spiritual gifts. Use them well to serve one another.
I PETER 4:10

Whatever gifts we have been given, we have been called to "use them well to serve one another" (1 Peter 4:10). How are you using the gifts God has given you? How are you encouraging your spouse's gifts?

Embracing Differences

Thank you for making me so wonderfully complex!
*   Your workmanship is marvelous—how well I know it.*
PSALM 139:14

The human body has many parts, but the many parts make
up one whole body. So it is with the body of Christ. . . . God
has put each part just where he wants it.
1 CORINTHIANS 12:12, 18

What do these passages show us about why we should
treat all people with respect?

Practically speaking, how could you implement some
of the principles from these verses in your marriage and
family life?

WRAPPING UP

What's one takeaway from this session you would like to focus on as a couple or as a family in the week ahead?

How can the rest of the group pray for you?

ON YOUR OWN

(To be completed after the session.)

* Is there something that has been pushed aside in your life or relationship that you want to make a priority? What's one thing you can do this week to give it the attention it deserves?

* Recall a time when your spouse showed that he or she was on your team. Encourage him or her by showing your appreciation for that moment.

* What's one way you are very different from your spouse? What's something good that comes as a result of that difference?

AN UNCOMMON COMMITMENT

//

BEFORE YOUR FOURTH SESSION

Read chapters 10–12 of *Uncommon Marriage*.

GETTING STARTED

The Newlywed/Oldly-wed Game

If you're part of a couples' small group, have one couple come to the front of the room and sit back-to-back. Have the couple write each of their names on separate pieces of paper. Designate another person in the group to read a few of the following statements out loud, starting each with "Which of you is more likely to . . . ?" For each question, the husband and wife will hold up one of the pieces of paper—with either their name or their spouse's name. Take time to compare if their answers matched, and then give the other couples a chance to participate.

If you're part of a men's or women's group, have each member take a look at the list below and write either their name or their spouse's name beside each item on the list. Next invite participants to talk about a time when one of those tendencies played out in a humorous or memorable way. When you get home, ask your spouse to answer "Which of you is more likely to . . ." for each item on the list, and then compare your answers.

Which of you is more likely to

steal the covers

talk in your sleep

put away the laundry

wash the dishes

be early

make a long-range plan

come home with a surprise

cook breakfast

read the instructions

introduce yourself to
   a stranger

tell a joke

get lost in a book

run out of gas

kill a spider

cry during a movie

be spontaneous

lose the keys

initiate a public display
   of affection

come up with an idea for
   a home-improvement
   project

sing in the shower

BUILDING AN UNCOMMON MARRIAGE

Using Your Gifts

God has given you and your spouse unique talents, abilities, and resources. When God brought the two of you together, He also brought together your own special combination of gifts. His desire is that the two of you will shine His light into the world as a dynamic team.

Since no two couples have the same gifts, their callings will play out in different ways too. For Lauren and Tony, a significant way they felt God calling them to use their gifts and resources was to raise a family and then expand it. They felt strongly that God had a clear plan for bringing each of their children into their family. Tony says: "I believe God put [our children] with us because He knew we would be able to take care of them. It was the perfect place for them to be, all part of His perfect plan" (ch. 10).

Tony adds that adoption was a way for them to share what God had generously given to them: "God was allowing us to use our gifts and resources in a way that glorified Him. Lauren said it was as if God was allowing us to be a part of His Kingdom building" (ch. 10).

1. What gifts and resources do you have as a couple? What are some ways your gifts work well together?

2. What are some ways you might be able to use your unique talents and circumstances to build God's Kingdom?

Resolving Conflict

Conflict is an inevitable part of every relationship. A healthy marriage is not one that is free of conflict; rather, it's one in which both people can communicate their feelings and thoughts in the face of change and disagreement. Ultimately, working through conflict together in a constructive way can strengthen your relationship instead of pulling you apart.

The Dungys knew that the most important part of resolving conflict was communicating frequently and sharing their thoughts and feelings with each other. But they also learned how important it was to find the right time and place to communicate about a difficult topic: "We both know the biblical mandate not to go to bed angry. Ephesians 4:26 says, 'Don't sin by letting anger control you. Don't let the sun go down while you are still angry.' While some people view that as a hard-and-fast rule to resolve conflict immediately, we came to realize that there are times when just agreeing to disagree until the morning is the wiser course. It's not that we want a disagreement to linger or fester, but sometimes discretion seems to be the better part of valor" (ch. 11).

3. When you were growing up, how did your family deal with conflict?

4. When you and your spouse deal with conflict, are there certain times or places that are better to discuss it? Explain.

Staying Committed

In Scripture, a strong relationship is depicted as "a triple-braided cord" that is not easily broken (Ecclesiastes 4:12). But unity doesn't happen automatically the day you say "I do"; it's something married couples have to tend and fortify, or that cord may fray with the pressures of life.

Tony emphasizes that although feelings may change, commitment keeps a relationship solid: "As Lauren and I discovered, marital love matures and deepens over the years. To endure, it's got to be built on a solid commitment to the other person and the life you've built with each other rather than on your feelings, which may go up and down" (ch. 11).

It's especially important that we have that foundation of commitment to lean on when we face difficult times. Lauren says that after the death of Tony's dad and her own sudden illness, she and Tony "became even more committed to talking to our children about the importance of family relationships and the need to cherish every moment with one another. We knew the Bible says that tomorrow is not promised us, and these crises caused that truth to hit home for all of us" (ch. 12).

5. What do you think it means to have a relationship that is as strong as a triple-braided cord?

6. Have you ever been given advice on the role of feelings in a relationship? What role do you think feelings play?

Supporting Each Other

Not only do circumstances change over the course of marriage, but we ourselves change too. Author and theologian Lewis Smedes says, "My wife has lived with at least five different men since we were wed—and each of the five has been me." It's important to be attuned to your spouse and find ways to support him or her as you go through various stages.

Lauren talks about the importance of being there to support her husband after a football loss: "I wanted to consistently show my support for him, win or lose. And we did get slaughtered some games. But Tony knew that after he met with the team and did his interviews, [the children and I would] be outside the locker room waiting for him" (ch. 12). Tony felt that support, and it gave him confidence to do his best, no matter the win-loss record: "I've always known Lauren was my biggest fan, and she shows it over and over, in ways both big and small" (ch. 12).

While a spouse's support and encouragement can be one of the most powerful motivators in the world, the opposite is also true: destructive words from a spouse can hurt more than words from anyone else: "Hurtful words can be painful, no matter who they come from. But when they come from your spouse, the person you love so much, they hurt even more" (ch. 10).

7. Your spouse may not have a literal scoreboard that measures his or her success at the end of the day, but he or she does face losses in some form. What's one way you've found to show support for your spouse—a way to "wait outside the locker room" to show you're behind him or her?

LOOKING AT GOD'S WORD

Read these Scripture passages and discuss what they mean to you.

Using Your Gifts

No one lights a lamp and then puts it under a basket. Instead, a lamp is placed on a stand, where it gives light to everyone in the house.
MATTHEW 5:15

In his grace, God has given us different gifts for doing certain things well. So if God has given you the ability to prophesy, speak out with as much faith as God has given you.
ROMANS 12:6

Our gifts are not just for ourselves. Rather, as followers of Christ, each one of us is "a lamp . . . placed on a stand, where it gives light to everyone" (Matthew 5:15). What are some ways you might be able to use your unique talents and circumstances to reflect God's light to the world?

We have all been given "gifts for doing certain things well" (Romans 12:6). What gifts do you think God has given you as an individual?

Resolving Conflict

"Don't sin by letting anger control you." Don't let the sun go down while you are still angry, for anger gives a foothold to the devil.
EPHESIANS 4:26-27

Be like-minded, be sympathetic, love one another, be compassionate and humble.
1 PETER 3:8, NIV

In Ephesians 4:26-27, Paul tells us, "Don't let the sun go down while you are still angry, for anger gives a foothold to the devil." Why do you think the Bible offers such a strong warning against anger? If you have to briefly put off addressing a disagreement, how can you keep the devil from gaining a foothold in your heart?

Even when there's conflict, it's important that we follow the biblical command to "be like-minded, be sympathetic, love one another, be compassionate and humble" (1 Peter 3:8, NIV). What do you think it would look like to disagree and still demonstrate love and humility?

Staying Committed

Let your wife be a fountain of blessing for you.
    Rejoice in the wife of your youth.
PROVERBS 5:18

Make me truly happy by agreeing wholeheartedly with each other, loving one another, and working together with one mind and purpose.
PHILIPPIANS 2:2

Philippians 2:2 says that we are to love each other and to be "working together with one mind and purpose." What do you think it means for two different people to work together in this way?

Supporting Each Other

Love each other. Just as I have loved you, you should love each other.
JOHN 13:34

Share each other's burdens, and in this way obey the law of Christ.
GALATIANS 6:2

One way to support each other is to "share each other's burdens" (Galatians 6:2). What do you think it means to share your spouse's burdens? How could you be intentional about doing this on a regular basis?

Practically speaking, how could you implement some of the principles from these verses in your marriage and family life?

WRAPPING UP

What's one takeaway from this session you would like to focus on as a couple or as a family in the week ahead?

How can the rest of the group pray for you?

ON YOUR OWN

(To be completed after the session.)

* Affirm a gift you see in your spouse. Explain how you see it enriching you, your family, and/or the wider community.

* When you face conflict, what have you found to be the most constructive way to talk about it? What's the best time of day and location to discuss problems? What times or places are least conducive to resolving conflict?

* Ask your spouse what one thing you could do to support him or her this week.

AN UNCOMMON CALLING

//

BEFORE YOUR FIFTH SESSION

Read chapters 13–15 of *Uncommon Marriage*. Designate someone to bring note cards and writing utensils.

GETTING STARTED

Match-up Game

Distribute a note card to each person in the group. Have each person write down his or her answer to the following question: "When you were a child, what job did you want to have when you grew up?" Choose one person to collect all the cards and read them aloud. Then have everyone guess the person they think matches up with each answer. If times allows, you can play another round or two by answering "What was your first job?" or "What is your hidden talent?"

BUILDING AN UNCOMMON MARRIAGE

Going through Trials

At some point, crisis in some form will hit every marriage—often when we least expect it. And tragedy has the potential to rock a relationship, since each person grieves and processes differently. But with God's help, it's possible to find healing and extend grace to each other in the midst of pain.

When Tony and Lauren went through a season of deep sadness, they clung to God and to each other: "The pain and sorrow were indescribable, but because of our faith in God, we were able to hold on to our foundation—communication and prayer—through a very dark time" (ch. 13). As difficult as some of those days were, the Dungys remained grounded in their faith, which helped prevent tragedy from driving them apart. Lauren says, "We knew we weren't promised a life without trials, and we had to cling to God's promise that He was with us. We had to continue to hold on tightly to the Lord's presence in our lives and our commitment to each other" (ch. 13).

1. What trials have you gone through as a couple? How did you cope, both individually and together?

Discovering Your Calling

According to Frederick Buechner, "A marriage made in Heaven is one where a man and a woman become more richly themselves together than the chances are either of them could ever have managed to become alone." Not only do you have a unique calling as an individual, but you also have a calling as a married couple—a particular mission you can fulfill together.

Tony and Lauren learned that with so many requests and commitments competing for their attention, it was important for them to figure out what God had uniquely equipped and called them to do. They learned to ask, "What things can only you do?" (ch. 15). They also discovered that God gives us different callings for different seasons of life, depending on jobs, children, and life circumstances.

2. What do you think it means to have a calling as an individual? As a couple?

3. How has your involvement in various activities and commitments changed over the years, depending on your season in life?

When Opposites Attract

The old saying has been around almost as long as marriage itself: "Opposites attract." There's a lot of truth in that expression, and while differences can be a source of conflict, they don't have to drive us apart. In fact, they can be used by God to make us more effective as a team.

Tony says, "[Lauren's] philosophy and mine still give great balance to our marriage. We see, more clearly than ever, that some of our different perspectives came from our parents. I can't get mad at that or say Lauren should be more like me. That's one reason God brought us together, and we make good decisions when we work through things as a team" (ch. 15).

4. In what ways are you and your spouse opposites? How can that be an advantage?

5. What differences in perspective can you trace back to your family of origin?

Leaving a Legacy

The life of faith isn't so much a one-person sprint as a relay race. God has entrusted us with a baton, and He instructs us to pass it on to the next generation—whether that's our own children and grandchildren or children in our church or community.

Lauren and Tony know how important it is to model faith and healthy relationships for their own children, for the players they've mentored, and for the people with whom they regularly interact. Lauren says, "Because of what Tony and I have learned about the effect our family backgrounds had on each of us, we know that the way we relate to each other and the way we handle problems is serving as the blueprint for our own children" (ch. 15). Lauren and Tony believe that one of the most significant legacies they can leave behind is the blueprint for a strong marriage, which at a basic level can be boiled down to two principles: "Stay focused on each other" and "Let God lead your marriage."

6. Who is watching your marriage? Who are you leaving a legacy for?

7. What would you like people to remember you for after you're gone?

LOOKING AT GOD'S WORD

Read these Scripture passages and discuss what they mean to you.

Going through Trials

When troubles of any kind come your way, consider it an opportunity for great joy. For you know that when your faith is tested, your endurance has a chance to grow. So let it grow, for when your endurance is fully developed, you will be perfect and complete, needing nothing.

JAMES 1:2-4

These trials will show that your faith is genuine. It is being tested as fire tests and purifies gold—though your faith is far more precious than mere gold. So when your faith remains strong through many trials, it will bring you much praise and glory and honor on the day when Jesus Christ is revealed to the whole world.

1 PETER 1:7

James 1:2 says that we are to consider our trials "an opportunity for great joy" because trials strengthen our endurance in God. What do you think it means to consider hardship a great joy? What would this look like in your life and marriage?

We read in the Bible that trials test and purify us and "show that [our] faith is genuine" (1 Peter 1:7). In what ways have the trials you and your spouse endured tested or purified your marriage and your faith in God?

Discovering Your Calling

The Spirit of the Sovereign LORD is upon me,
*   for the LORD has anointed me*
*   to bring good news to the poor.*
He has sent me to comfort the brokenhearted
*   and to proclaim that captives will be released*
*   and prisoners will be freed.*
He has sent me to tell those who mourn
*   that the time of the LORD's favor has come.*
ISAIAH 61:1-2

Lead a life worthy of your calling, for you have been called
by God.
EPHESIANS 4:1

Ephesians 4:1 tells each of us to "lead a life worthy of [our] calling, for [we] have been called by God." What does it mean to lead a life worthy of our calling? How do you think this is done as an individual and as a couple?

When Opposites Attract

You made all the delicate, inner parts of my body
and knit me together in my mother's womb.
PSALM 139:13

The human body has many parts, but the many parts make
up one whole body. So it is with the body of Christ.
I CORINTHIANS 12:12

Even though you and your spouse may be opposite in some ways, both of you were crafted specifically by God (Psalm 139:13). How does that understanding help you appreciate people who are different from you—including your spouse?

First Corinthians 12:12 describes the community of Christ as a body made up of many parts, in which each part has an important function. Think about the ways you and your spouse are different. How do your unique perspectives enrich your life and your relationship?

Leaving a Legacy

We will not hide these truths from our children;
  we will tell the next generation
about the glorious deeds of the LORD,
  about his power and his mighty wonders.
PSALM 78:4

Direct your children onto the right path,
  and when they are older, they will not leave it.
PROVERBS 22:6

As Christians, we are instructed to pass on stories about "the glorious deeds of the LORD . . . his power and his mighty wonders" (Psalm 78:4). In your season of life, how can you, both as an individual and as a couple, spread the Good News about Jesus and God's love?

Proverbs 22:6 says, "Direct your children onto the right path, and when they are older, they will not leave it." In what ways did your parents or other adults direct you to the right path? How has your upbringing influenced your adult life and your marriage?

Practically speaking, how could you implement some of the principles from these verses in your marriage and family life?

WRAPPING UP

What's one takeaway from this session you would like to focus on as a couple or as a family in the week ahead?

How can the rest of the group pray for you?

ON YOUR OWN

(To be completed after the session.)

* What do you see as your calling—both individually and as a couple? Is there a passion you'd like to pursue as you seek to fulfill that calling?

* Write down the legacy you'd like to leave for the next generation.

* What have you learned as a result of completing this Bible study together?

LEADER'S GUIDE

This Bible study has been designed to make it easy for participants to read and engage with the material without a great deal of preparation on your part as the leader. Even so, it is helpful to have someone who can coordinate the logistics, facilitate conversation, and make sure the group stays on track. Every team—no matter how strong—needs a coach! If you are the leader of your group, thank you for your willingness to serve in this capacity.

As you read through this leader's guide, keep in mind that these tips are merely suggestions to help the sessions run smoothly. You know your group best, so feel free to adapt this study to meet these unique needs and to suit your own leadership style.

PURPOSE OF THIS STUDY

The members of your group may have different goals for being part of this study, and they may be in various places in their marriage. But there's one unifying goal you can focus on as a leader: to encourage each couple to grow in their relationship and develop healthy patterns so they can build and maintain an uncommon marriage.

LOGISTICS TO CONSIDER

Duration: This is a five-session study. Decide whether your group will meet weekly or every other week.

Materials: Each participant/couple will need the book *Uncommon Marriage* and this Bible study. Determine if people will buy their own books or if they'll be purchased by one point person.

Meeting details: Decide where and when you will meet and if child care will be provided. You might also want to consider if food/snacks will be part of each session.

Contact information: You may want to get the phone numbers and/or e-mail addresses for the members of your group in case you need to communicate with people throughout the week.

Discussion format: There are many ways to facilitate discussion using the Bible study, depending on the needs and desires of your group. You may encourage participants to read the content for each session ahead of time and answer the questions in advance. Or you might want to have group members read the content and questions during the meeting—either out loud or on their own.

TIPS FOR LEADERS

Pray for the group before each session, asking God to prepare people's hearts to be touched and to bless each relationship represented.

As you facilitate conversation in your group, be aware that some people may tend to dominate the discussion while others may remain quiet. Try to pay attention to the dynamics so you can redirect the discussion as needed and invite everyone to participate.

Create a safe environment for participants to share openly. You may want to remind group members that the things shared in your group are confidential. Be sure to set a tone of grace as people open up about their relationships and their struggles.

* If any group members share something about
their marriage that seems to go beyond your scope
as a leader (such as abuse, infidelity, or clinical
depression), refer them to a pastor or a Christian
counselor.

ANSWER KEY

From Session 3: The Battle of the Sexes

1.	b	6.	c
2.	d	7.	d
3.	a	8.	c
4.	c	9.	b
5.	d	10.	b

Thank you for investing in your group as you embark
on this journey toward an uncommon marriage together!

ENDNOTES

page 17   C. S. Lewis, *Mere Christianity* (New York: HarperCollins, 2009), 110.

page 36   Mike Mason, *The Mystery of Marriage* (Colorado Springs, CO: Multnomah, 2005), 14.

page 55   Timothy Keller, *The Meaning of Marriage* (New York: Riverhead Books, 2011), 100–101.

page 59   Billy Graham, *Just As I Am: The Autobiography of Billy Graham* (New York: HarperCollins, 1997), 714.

page 77   Quoted in Keller's, *The Meaning of Marriage*, 97.

page 89   Frederick Buechner, *Whistling in the Dark: A Doubter's Dictionary* (New York: HarperCollins, 1993), 87.

Tony Dungy is the #1 *New York Times* bestselling author of *Quiet Strength*, *Uncommon*, *The Mentor Leader*, and *The One Year Uncommon Life Daily Challenge*. He led the Indianapolis Colts to Super Bowl victory on February 4, 2007, the first such win for an African American head coach. Dungy established another NFL first by becoming the first head coach to lead his teams to the playoffs for ten consecutive years. He retired from coaching in 2009 and now serves as a studio analyst for NBC's *Football Night in America*. He is dedicated to mentoring others, especially young people, and encouraging them to live uncommon lives.

Lauren Dungy is an early childhood specialist and a bestselling children's book author. She serves as vice president of the Dungy Family Foundation, which helps meet the spiritual, social, and educational needs of those in her community. Lauren is also a national spokesperson for the iMom organization. She is involved in many charitable causes in the Tampa area, which revolve around three central themes—Christian outreach, children, and education. The Dungys are the parents of nine children.

Nathan Whitaker holds degrees from Duke University, Harvard Law School, and the University of Florida and has worked in football administration for the Jacksonville Jaguars and Tampa Bay Buccaneers. He has written six *New York Times* bestsellers and lives with his family in Florida.

Stephanie Rische is a senior editor of nonfiction books at Tyndale House Publishers, as well as a freelance writer for various publications, including *Today's Christian Woman*, *Significant Living* magazine, *Marriage Partnership*, and *her.meneutics*. She and her husband, Daniel, live in the Chicago area, where they enjoy riding their bikes, making homemade ice cream, and swapping bad puns.

BRING *UNCOMMON MARRIAGE* TO YOUR CHURCH!

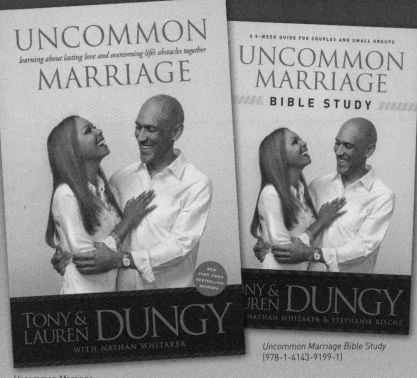

Uncommon Marriage Bible Study
(978-1-4143-9199-1)

Uncommon Marriage
Hardcover (978-1-4143-8369-9)
Audio CDs read by Tony and Lauren Dungy (978-1-4143-8371-2)

For free resources to host an Uncommon Marriage Month at your church, visit **www.coachdungy.com**.

Free downloadable materials for a 5-week event include:
- Sermon notes
- Video promos
- Topical video introductions for each week
- Guide for event leaders
- Supplemental discussion guides for "men's only" and "women's only" groups
- Promotional artwork for signs, posters, bulletin inserts, websites, and e-mails

CP0734

ALSO FROM TONY DUNGY AND TYNDALE MOMENTUM

Quiet Strength
Uncommon
The Mentor Leader
The One Year Uncommon Life Daily Challenge
Uncommon Manhood (gift book)
Tony Dungy on Winning with Quiet Strength (DVD)
Dare to Be Uncommon (DVD)

CHILDREN'S BOOKS BY TONY & LAUREN DUNGY
(AVAILABLE THROUGH SIMON & SCHUSTER)

You Can Do It!
You Can Be a Friend
The Missing Cupcake Mystery
A Team Stays Together!
Justin and the Bully
Go, Jade, Go!
Ruby's New Home